THANKSGIVING

by Charly Haley

Cody Koala

An Imprint of Pop!

popbooksonline.com

abdobooks.com

Published by Pop!, a division of ABDO, PO Box 398166, Minneapolis, Minnesota 55439. Copyright © 2019 by POP, LLC. International copyrights reserved in all countries. No part of this book may be reproduced in any form without written permission from the publisher. Pop!™ is a trademark and logo of POP, LLC.

Printed in the United States of America, North Mankato, Minnesota

082018
012019

THIS BOOK CONTAINS RECYCLED MATERIALS

Cover Photo: iStockphoto

Interior Photos: iStockphoto, 1, 9 (top), 19, 20; Shutterstock Images, 5, 7, 9 (bottom left), 9 (bottom right), 10, 11, 13, 16, 17; North Wind Picture Archives, 14, 15

Editor: Meg Gaertner
Series Designer: Laura Mitchell

Library of Congress Control Number: 2018949961

Publisher's Cataloging-in-Publication Data

Names: Haley, Charly, author.
Title: Thanksgiving / by Charly Haley.
Description: Minneapolis, Minnesota : Pop!, 2019 | Series: Holidays | Includes online resources and index.
Identifiers: ISBN 9781532162008 (lib. bdg.) | ISBN 9781641855716 (pbk) | ISBN 9781532163067 (ebook)
Subjects: LCSH: Thanksgiving--Juvenile literature. | Holidays--Juvenile literature. | National holidays--Juvenile literature.
Classification: DDC 394.2649--dc23

Hello! My name is

Cody Koala

Pop open this book and you'll find QR codes like this one, loaded with information, so you can learn even more!

Scan this code* and others like it while you read, or visit the website below to make this book pop.

popbooksonline.com/thanksgiving

*Scanning QR codes requires a web-enabled smart device with a QR code reader app and a camera.

Table of Contents

Chapter 1

Thanksgiving

Family and friends share a large meal. They think about what they are thankful for. It is Thanksgiving.

Watch a video here!

Thanksgiving in the United States happens in November. It is celebrated on the fourth Thursday. It is a day to be thankful.

Thanksgiving became a US national holiday in 1863.

November

Mon	Tue	Wed	Thu	Fri	Sat	Sun
						1
2	3	4	5	6	7	8
9	10	11	12	13	14	15
16	17	18	19	20	21	22
23	24	25	26	27	28	29
30						

Chapter 2

Harvest

The Thanksgiving **tradition** is to eat a large family meal. The **feast** often includes turkey, potatoes, and pie for dessert. Each family may have its own traditions.

Learn more here!

Fall is known as the season of **harvest**. Today farmers still gather **crops** in the fall.

The large meal on
Thanksgiving is to celebrate
a good harvest.

Chapter 3

History

People believe the first Thanksgiving celebration happened in 1621. **Colonists** and Native Americans shared a meal to celebrate the harvest.

Learn more here!

Colonists came to
America from Europe.
But Native Americans lived
in America first.

Colonists killed many
Native Americans and took
their land.

Today many Native Americans ask people to remember this history.

People can learn about

different Native American

tribes. They can celebrate

the traditions of these tribes.

Chapter 4

Celebrations

The most famous part of Thanksgiving celebrations is the feast. Some people even call Thanksgiving "Turkey Day."

Complete an activity here!

But the important part of Thanksgiving is being thankful. Some people will tell each other what they are thankful for. They spend time together on the holiday.

Many countries have holidays to celebrate being thankful.

Making Connections

Text-to-Self

Have you ever celebrated Thanksgiving with your family? Who came to the meal? What did you eat?

Text-to-Text

Have you read any other books about holidays? What did you learn?

Text-to-World

Thanksgiving is a day to celebrate being thankful. What things in the world are you thankful for?

Glossary

colonist – someone who settles in a new area but is supported by his or her original country.

crop – a plant grown by farmers, usually for food.

feast – a large meal with many different foods.

harvest – to gather or pick crops.

tradition – a belief or way of doing things that is passed down from person to person over time.

tribe – a group of people with shared history and beliefs who live and work together.

Index

Online Resources

popbooksonline.com

Thanks for reading this Cody Koala book!

Scan this code* and others like it in this book, or visit the website below to make this book pop!

popbooksonline.com/thanksgiving

*Scanning QR codes requires a web-enabled smart device with a QR code reader app and a camera.